Introduction

Sustainable investing and impactful philanthropy are two powerful tools that individuals and organizations can use to drive positive social and environmental change. In this comprehensive guide, we will explore what sustainable investing and impactful philanthropy are, how they work, and how to get started.

Chapter 1: Understanding Sustainable Investing

1.1 What is Sustainable Investing?
1.2 Why is Sustainable Investing Important?
1.3 Sustainable Investing Strategies
1.4 ESG Investing
1.5 Impact Investing
1.6 Green Bonds and Sustainable Fixed Income
1.7 Key Considerations for Sustainable Investing
1.8 Measuring the Impact of Sustainable Investing

1.9 Getting Started with Sustainable Investing

Chapter 2: Understanding Impactful Philanthropy

2.1 What is Philanthropy?
2.2 Why is Philanthropy Important?
2.3 Types of Philanthropy
2.4 Measuring the Impact of Philanthropy
2.5 Giving Strategically
2.6 Key Considerations for Impactful Philanthropy

2.7 Getting Started with Impactful Philanthropy

Chapter 3: The Intersection of Sustainable Investing and Impactful Philanthropy

3.1 What is the Intersection of Sustainable Investing and Impactful Philanthropy?
3.2 How to Incorporate Sustainable Investing into Philanthropy
3.3 How to Incorporate Philanthropy into Sustainable Investing

3.4 Key Considerations for Combining Sustainable Investing and Impactful Philanthropy

Conclusion

Sustainable investing and impactful philanthropy are two powerful tools that can be used to drive positive social and environmental change. By understanding how sustainable investing and philanthropy work, and by building sustainable portfolios and measuring impact, individuals and organizations can make a meaningful difference in the world. Use the resources provided in this guide to get started on your journey towards making a positive impact.

Chapter 1: Understanding Sustainable Investing

Chapter 1: Understanding Sustainable Investing

1.1 What is Sustainable Investing?

Sustainable investing is an investment approach that seeks to generate financial returns while promoting social and environmental sustainability. It involves investing in companies or projects that prioritize sustainability and environmental stewardship, while also considering social and governance factors.

Sustainable investing can take many forms, including ESG (Environmental, Social, and Governance) investing, impact investing, and green bonds. Sustainable investing aims to achieve a positive impact on the environment and society while also generating financial returns for investors.

1.2 Why is Sustainable Investing Important?

Sustainable investing is important for several reasons. Firstly, it can promote social and environmental sustainability, which can lead to a healthier planet and a better quality of life for all people. Additionally, sustainable investing can help investors achieve their financial goals while also promoting positive social and environmental outcomes.

Moreover, sustainable investing is increasingly popular with investors, and many studies have shown that companies with high sustainability ratings tend to outperform their peers over the long-term. As more investors embrace sustainable investing, it is likely that sustainable investments will become more prevalent and mainstream.

1.3 Sustainable Investing Strategies

Sustainable investing strategies vary depending on the investment goals of the investor. Some common sustainable investing strategies include:

- Negative screening: excluding companies or industries that have negative social or environmental impacts.
- Positive screening: including companies or industries that have positive social or environmental impacts.
- ESG integration: analyzing companies based on their environmental, social, and governance (ESG) performance and integrating this analysis into investment decisions.
- Impact investing: investing in companies or projects that have a measurable positive impact on society or the environment.
- Shareholder engagement: engaging with companies to promote positive social and environmental outcomes.
- Thematic investing: investing in companies that are aligned with a particular theme, such as clean energy or sustainable agriculture.

1.4 ESG Investing

ESG investing is an investment approach that considers the environmental, social, and governance performance of companies. It involves analyzing companies based on their performance in areas such as carbon emissions, water usage, human rights, labor practices, executive compensation, and board diversity. ESG investing aims to identify companies that prioritize sustainability and environmental stewardship, while also considering social and governance factors.

ESG investing can be applied to various investment strategies, including negative screening, positive screening, and ESG integration. Companies that perform well on ESG factors may be more likely to generate long-term value for investors and avoid risks related to environmental or social issues.

1.5 Impact Investing

Impact investing involves investing in companies or projects that have a measurable positive impact on society or the environment. Impact investments may be made in a wide range of industries, including renewable energy, sustainable agriculture, and affordable housing. The goal of impact investing is to generate financial returns while also promoting positive social or environmental outcomes.

Impact investing is a growing field, and it is estimated that the market for impact investments will continue to grow in the coming years. Impact investing may involve various investment strategies, including private equity, venture capital, and fixed income investments.

1.6 Green Bonds and Sustainable Fixed Income

Green bonds are fixed-income securities that are issued to finance environmentally friendly projects. The proceeds from green bonds may be used to finance projects such as renewable energy, energy efficiency, or sustainable agriculture. Green bonds provide investors with an opportunity to invest in projects that promote environmental sustainability while also generating financial returns.

Sustainable fixed income investments may also include social bonds, which finance projects that promote social outcomes such as affordable housing or healthcare. Sustainable fixed income investments are a growing area of the sustainable investing market and may provide investors with a range of investment options.

1.7 Key Considerations for Sustainable Investing

When considering sustainable investing, investors should consider several key factors, including: Investment goals

Chapter 2: Understanding Impactful Philanthropy

Chapter 2: Understanding Impactful Philanthropy

2.1 What is Philanthropy?

Philanthropy is the practice of giving time, money, or resources for the purpose of promoting social and environmental goals. Philanthropy is a form of voluntary action that seeks to improve the well-being of others and to create positive social change.

Philanthropy can take many forms, including donating money to charities or non-profit organizations, volunteering time to a cause, or supporting social and environmental initiatives through business or personal investments.

2.2 Why is Philanthropy Important?

Philanthropy is important for several reasons. Firstly, it can help to address social and environmental issues that may not be adequately addressed by government or market forces. Philanthropy can also provide resources to organizations that are working to promote positive social change, and it can help to create a culture of giving and social responsibility.

Moreover, philanthropy can provide individuals and organizations with a sense of purpose and satisfaction, as they contribute to causes that are meaningful to them. Philanthropy can also help to build relationships and networks, both within the philanthropic community and with the organizations that are being supported.

2.3 Types of Philanthropy

Philanthropy can take many forms, including:

- Donating money: giving money to charities or non-profit organizations.
- Volunteering time: providing time and expertise to a cause or organization.
- In-kind giving: donating goods or services to a cause or organization.
- Socially responsible investing: investing in companies or projects that prioritize social and environmental outcomes.
- Impact investing: investing in companies or projects that have a measurable positive impact on society or the environment.

2.4 Measuring the Impact of Philanthropy

Measuring the impact of philanthropy can be challenging, as social and environmental outcomes may be difficult to quantify or attribute to a particular intervention. However, there are several methods for measuring the impact of philanthropy, including:

- Output measures: measuring the number of people reached or services provided by a particular intervention.
- Outcome measures: measuring changes in behavior or attitudes as a result of a particular intervention.
- Impact assessment: conducting a comprehensive assessment of the social or environmental impact of a particular intervention.

It is important to consider the appropriate method for measuring the impact of philanthropy, based on the goals of the intervention and the nature of the issue being addressed.

2.5 Giving Strategically

Giving strategically involves identifying the most effective ways to achieve social or environmental outcomes through philanthropy. Some key strategies for giving strategically include:

- Identifying high-impact areas: identifying areas where philanthropic interventions can have the most impact, such as health, education, or environmental conservation.
- Collaboration: working with other philanthropists or organizations to maximize impact and avoid duplication of efforts.
- Evidence-based giving: supporting interventions that have been shown to be effective through rigorous evaluation and research.
- Capacity building: supporting organizations to build their capacity to achieve their goals more effectively.

Giving strategically requires careful planning and consideration of the most effective ways to achieve social and environmental outcomes through philanthropy.

2.6 Key Considerations for Impactful Philanthropy

When considering impactful philanthropy, it is important to consider several key factors, including:

- Identifying philanthropic goals: identifying the social or environmental outcomes that the philanthropy aims to achieve.
- Assessing the impact of interventions: evaluating the effectiveness of interventions in achieving the desired outcomes.
- Building relationships: building relationships with organizations and communities to better understand their needs and priorities.
- Measuring impact: measuring the impact of philanthropy to ensure that interventions are achieving the desired outcomes.
- Continual learning: continually learning and adapting to maximize impact and address emerging challenges.

2.7 Getting Started with Impactful Philanthropy

Getting started with impactful philanthropy involves

Chapter 3: The Intersection of Sustainable Investing and Impactful Philanthropy

3.1 What is the Intersection of Sustainable Investing and Impactful Philanthropy?

The intersection of sustainable investing and impactful philanthropy refers to the practice of using investment strategies and philanthropic giving to achieve positive social and environmental outcomes. The intersection of these two practices recognizes that both investment and philanthropy can be powerful tools for creating positive change and that they can work together to achieve greater impact.

Sustainable investing and impactful philanthropy can complement each other by leveraging different approaches to social and environmental change. Sustainable investing focuses on integrating environmental, social, and governance (ESG) considerations into investment decisions, while impactful philanthropy aims to support social and environmental initiatives through charitable giving. When combined, these two practices can create a powerful approach to achieving positive outcomes.

3.2 How to Incorporate Sustainable Investing into Philanthropy

Incorporating sustainable investing into philanthropy involves investing in companies and projects that align with the philanthropic goals and values of the donor. This can be achieved in several ways, including:

- Investing in impact funds: Impact funds are investment funds that focus on generating positive social and environmental outcomes alongside financial returns. Investing in impact funds can provide philanthropists with a way to invest in companies and projects that align with their philanthropic goals.

- Screening investments: Philanthropists can screen their investments to ensure that they align with their values and goals. This can involve excluding companies that engage in practices that conflict with philanthropic goals, such as companies that produce fossil fuels or engage in human rights abuses.
- Using shareholder advocacy: Philanthropists can use their shareholder influence to advocate for companies to improve their environmental, social, and governance (ESG) practices. This can involve engaging with companies through shareholder resolutions and voting on key issues.

3.3 How to Incorporate Philanthropy into Sustainable Investing

Incorporating philanthropy into sustainable investing involves identifying opportunities to support social and environmental initiatives through investment. This can be achieved in several ways, including:

- Impact investing: Impact investing involves investing in companies or projects that have a measurable positive impact on society or the environment. Impact investing can be a powerful tool for achieving philanthropic goals through investment.
- Socially responsible investing: Socially responsible investing involves investing in companies that prioritize ESG considerations alongside financial returns. This can provide philanthropists with a way to support companies that align with their philanthropic goals while generating financial returns.
- ESG integration: ESG integration involves integrating environmental, social, and governance considerations into investment decisions. This can provide philanthropists with a way to support companies that prioritize ESG considerations, while also generating financial returns.

3.4 Key Considerations for Combining Sustainable Investing and Impactful Philanthropy

When combining sustainable investing and impactful philanthropy, it is important to consider several key factors, including:

- Alignment of goals: It is important to ensure that sustainable investing and philanthropic goals are aligned and that they support each other. This can involve identifying areas of overlap and prioritizing initiatives that achieve both financial and social or environmental outcomes.

- Due diligence: Due diligence is important to ensure that investment opportunities align with philanthropic goals and values. This can involve assessing the impact of investments and the practices of companies and projects.
- Measurement of impact: It is important to measure the impact of both sustainable investing and philanthropic initiatives to ensure that they are achieving the desired outcomes. This can involve assessing financial, social, and environmental outcomes and adjusting strategies accordingly.
- Collaboration: Collaboration with other investors and philanthropists can help to achieve greater impact and avoid duplication of efforts. Collaboration can also help to identify new investment opportunities and philanthropic initiatives.

Chapter 4: Building a Sustainable Portfolio

Chapter 4: Building a Sustainable Portfolio

4.1 The Importance of Building a Sustainable Portfolio

Building a sustainable portfolio involves investing in companies and projects that prioritize environmental, social, and governance (ESG) considerations. Sustainable investing is becoming increasingly popular as investors recognize the importance of investing in companies and projects that contribute to a sustainable future. Building a sustainable portfolio is important for several reasons:

- Positive impact: Investing in companies and projects that prioritize ESG considerations can create positive social and environmental impact, making a tangible difference in the world.
- Risk management: Investing in companies with strong ESG practices can reduce the risk of negative events that can harm both financial performance and the environment.
- Future proofing: As the world shifts towards a more sustainable future, companies with strong ESG practices are better positioned to adapt to new regulations and market trends.

4.2 How to Build a Sustainable Portfolio

Building a sustainable portfolio involves identifying companies and projects that prioritize ESG considerations and integrating them into an investment strategy. This can be achieved in several ways, including:

- Investing in ESG funds: ESG funds are investment funds that prioritize ESG considerations in their investment decisions. Investing in ESG funds can provide exposure to companies and projects with strong ESG practices.
- Screening investments: Investors can screen their investments to ensure that they align with their values and goals. This can involve excluding companies that engage in practices that conflict with ESG goals, such as companies that produce fossil fuels or engage in human rights abuses.
- Using ESG ratings: ESG ratings are used to assess the environmental, social, and governance practices of companies. Using ESG ratings can help investors identify companies with strong ESG practices and integrate them into an investment strategy.

4.3 Sustainable Investing and Diversification

Diversification is an important consideration when building a sustainable portfolio. Diversification involves spreading investments across a range of companies and projects to reduce risk.

Sustainable investing can be incorporated into a diversified investment strategy in several ways:

- Investing in multiple ESG funds: Investing in multiple ESG funds can provide exposure to a range of companies and projects with strong ESG practices.
- Screening investments across a range of sectors: Screening investments across a range of sectors can help investors identify companies with strong ESG practices in a variety of industries.
- Incorporating ESG considerations into traditional investment strategies: ESG considerations can be incorporated into traditional investment strategies to create a diversified portfolio that includes companies with strong ESG practices.

4.4 Sustainable Investing and Risk Management

Sustainable investing can help to manage investment risk by identifying companies and projects with strong ESG practices. Companies with strong ESG practices are better positioned to manage risk in several ways:

- Reduced regulatory risk: Companies with strong ESG practices are better positioned to adapt to changing regulations and market trends, reducing regulatory risk.
- Improved supply chain management: Companies with strong ESG practices are better positioned to manage their supply chains, reducing the risk of supply chain disruptions.

- Improved brand reputation: Companies with strong ESG practices are less likely to face reputational damage from negative environmental or social events, reducing brand risk.

4.5 Sustainable Investing and Financial Performance

Sustainable investing can deliver strong financial performance while also achieving positive social and environmental outcomes. Research has shown that companies with strong ESG practices can outperform those with weaker ESG practices in several ways:

- Lower cost of capital: Companies with strong ESG practices may have lower borrowing costs due to reduced risk.
- Increased innovation: Companies with strong ESG practices may be more innovative, creating new products and services that can drive financial performance.
- Increased customer loyalty: Companies with strong ESG practices may have higher levels of customer loyalty due to their positive environmental and social impact.

4.6 Key Considerations for Building a Sustainable Portfolio

Chapter 5: Measuring the Impact of Sustainable Investing and Philanthropy

Chapter 5: Measuring the Impact of Sustainable Investing and Philanthropy

5.1 The Importance of Measuring Impact

Measuring the impact of sustainable investing and philanthropy is crucial to ensure that these activities are fulfilling their intended purpose. Impact measurement helps to determine the effectiveness of investments and philanthropic donations in creating positive social, environmental, and financial outcomes. Measuring the impact of sustainable investing and philanthropy is also essential for transparency and accountability, as it helps investors and philanthropists to understand the real-world impact of their actions and make data-driven decisions for the future.

5.2 Common Metrics for Measuring Impact

There are many metrics that investors and philanthropists can use to measure the impact of their actions. Some of the most common metrics include:

- Environmental Impact: Metrics such as carbon footprint, water usage, and waste reduction are used to measure the environmental impact of sustainable investments and philanthropic initiatives.
- Social Impact: Metrics such as employment generation, access to education, and community development are used to measure the social impact of investments and philanthropy.
- Financial Impact: Metrics such as return on investment (ROI) and net present value (NPV) are used to measure the financial impact of sustainable investments.
- Impact on Sustainable Development Goals (SDGs): The United Nations Sustainable Development Goals (SDGs) provide a framework for measuring the impact of investments and philanthropy on social and environmental issues. Metrics such as the number of people lifted out of poverty, access to healthcare, and access to clean water can be used to measure the impact on SDGs.

5.3 Impact Measurement for Sustainable Investing

Measuring the impact of sustainable investments can be challenging, as it requires investors to go beyond traditional financial metrics and evaluate non-financial factors such as social and environmental impact. To measure the impact of sustainable investments, investors can use a variety of methods, including:

- Data Analysis: Investors can analyze data from companies and organizations to understand their impact on the environment and society. This can include data on carbon emissions, water usage, waste management, and labor practices.
- Third-Party Ratings: Investors can use third-party ratings agencies to evaluate the sustainability of companies and investments. These agencies assess companies and investments based on a range of sustainability factors, including environmental impact, social responsibility, and corporate governance.
- Impact Investing Funds: Investors can invest in impact investing funds, which are designed to generate both financial returns and positive social and environmental outcomes. These funds typically focus on specific social or environmental issues, such as clean energy, affordable housing, or healthcare.

5.4 Impact Measurement for Philanthropy

Measuring the impact of philanthropic initiatives can be challenging, as it requires philanthropists to evaluate the effectiveness of their donations in creating positive social and environmental outcomes. To measure the impact of philanthropic initiatives, philanthropists can use a variety of methods, including:

- Grant Evaluations: Philanthropists can evaluate the impact of their grants by tracking the progress of the organizations that receive them. This can involve reviewing reports and data from the organizations, as well as conducting site visits and interviews with stakeholders.
- Social Return on Investment (SROI): SROI is a framework for measuring the social, environmental, and financial impact of philanthropic initiatives. It involves assigning a monetary value to the outcomes of philanthropic initiatives, such as increased access to education or improved health outcomes.

- Randomized Controlled Trials (RCTs): RCTs are a scientific method for evaluating the impact of interventions on social and environmental outcomes. Philanthropists can use RCTs to evaluate the impact of their donations in a rigorous and systematic way.

Chapter 6: Case Studies of Sustainable Investing and Philanthropy

Chapter 6: Case Studies of Sustainable Investing and Philanthropy

Real-life examples of sustainable investing and impactful philanthropy can help investors and donors better understand how to put theory into practice. In this chapter, we will examine several case studies that demonstrate the effectiveness of these practices and their ability to create positive change in the world.

6.1 Sustainable Investing Case Studies

6.1.1 Calvert Investments

Calvert Investments is a socially responsible investment management company that uses a range of strategies to invest in companies that have a positive impact on society and the environment. They have been recognized for their work in sustainable investing, having been named one of the world's most ethical companies by Ethisphere for 11 consecutive years.

Calvert has a number of mutual funds that invest in companies with strong environmental, social, and governance (ESG) performance, including the Calvert Equity Fund, which has a long history of outperforming its benchmark. The Calvert Green Bond Fund invests in bonds issued to finance climate solutions, such as renewable energy and energy efficiency projects.

6.1.2 Impax Asset Management

Impax Asset Management is an investment management company that specializes in sustainable investing. They focus on investing in companies that are driving the transition to a more sustainable economy, such as those involved in renewable energy, energy efficiency, and water management.

Impax has a range of mutual funds that invest in sustainable companies, including the Impax Environmental Markets (IEM) fund, which invests in companies that provide solutions to environmental challenges. The IEM fund has delivered strong long-term performance, outperforming its benchmark by more than 5% per year since its launch.

6.2 Philanthropy Case Studies

6.2.1 The Bill and Melinda Gates Foundation

The Bill and Melinda Gates Foundation is one of the largest private charitable foundations in the world. Its mission is to improve global health and reduce poverty through philanthropy. The foundation has committed over $50 billion to a range of initiatives, including vaccine development, global health, and education.

One of the foundation's most successful initiatives has been its work on global health, including efforts to combat infectious diseases such as HIV/AIDS, tuberculosis, and malaria. The foundation has committed more than $10 billion to these efforts and has been credited with helping to save millions of lives.

6.2.2 The Chan Zuckerberg Initiative

The Chan Zuckerberg Initiative is a philanthropic organization founded by Facebook CEO Mark Zuckerberg and his wife Priscilla Chan. The organization's mission is to advance human potential and promote equality. It has committed over $1.6 billion to a range of initiatives, including education, scientific research, and affordable housing.

One of the initiative's flagship projects is the Biohub, a research collaboration between Stanford University, the University of California, San Francisco, and the University of California, Berkeley. The Biohub focuses on developing new technologies for curing diseases and improving human health.

6.3 Intersection of Sustainable Investing and Philanthropy Case Studies

6.3.1 The Rockefeller Foundation

The Rockefeller Foundation is a philanthropic organization that works to promote the well-being of humanity throughout the world. The foundation has a long history of supporting sustainable development and has committed over $2 billion to initiatives aimed at promoting sustainable agriculture, clean energy, and resilience to climate change.

The foundation also has an impact investing arm, the Rockefeller Foundation Impact Investment Management (RFIIM), which invests in companies and funds that have a positive social or environmental impact. One of RFIIM's successful investments has been in Leapfrog Investments, a private equity firm that invests in companies that provide financial services to underserved populations in Africa and Asia.

Chapter Chapter 7: Resources for Sustainable Investing and Philanthropy

Chapter 7: Resources for Sustainable Investing and Philanthropy

Investors and philanthropists looking to engage in sustainable investing and impactful philanthropy have access to a wide range of resources to help guide their decision-making and actions. These resources include tools, frameworks, data sources, networks, and organizations that provide guidance and support for sustainable investing and philanthropy.

7.1 Sustainable Investing Resources

Sustainable investing resources include organizations, data sources, frameworks, and tools that can help investors incorporate ESG factors and impact investing into their investment decision-making process. Here are some resources that investors can use:

- The United Nations Principles for Responsible Investment (PRI): The PRI is a network of investors committed to incorporating ESG factors into their investment decisions. The PRI provides a framework for investors to incorporate sustainability factors into their investment analysis, decision-making, and ownership practices.
- MSCI ESG Research: MSCI ESG Research provides ESG ratings and data on thousands of companies worldwide. Investors can use this data to evaluate companies' ESG risks and opportunities and make informed investment decisions.
- CDP: CDP is a global non-profit organization that provides environmental disclosure and data for companies, cities, and states. Investors can use this data to assess companies' environmental performance and risks.
- Global Impact Investing Network (GIIN): GIIN is a non-profit organization that promotes impact investing globally. The GIIN provides a range of resources, including standards and best practices for impact investing, data on impact investments, and a network of impact investors.
- Sustainability Accounting Standards Board (SASB): The SASB is an independent organization that provides industry-specific ESG standards for companies. These standards can help investors evaluate ESG risks and opportunities and compare companies' sustainability performance across industries.

- Carbon Disclosure Project (CDP): The CDP provides environmental data and disclosure for companies around the world. Investors can use this data to evaluate companies' carbon footprint and develop strategies to mitigate climate change risk.

7.2 Philanthropy Resources

Philanthropy resources include organizations, tools, and frameworks that can help philanthropists maximize the impact of their charitable giving. Here are some resources that philanthropists can use:

- Giving Compass: Giving Compass is an online platform that provides resources, tools, and information for effective philanthropy. The platform provides guidance on how to identify and support high-impact philanthropic initiatives.
- Philanthropy University: Philanthropy University is an online learning platform that provides free courses and resources on effective philanthropy. The platform covers a range of topics, including impact measurement, fundraising, and grant-making.
- GuideStar: GuideStar is a database of over 2.5 million non-profit organizations. Philanthropists can use GuideStar to research and evaluate non-profit organizations, including their mission, programs, finances, and impact.
- The Center for Effective Philanthropy (CEP): The CEP is a non-profit organization that provides research, tools, and resources to help philanthropists improve their impact. The CEP provides guidance on effective grant-making, impact measurement, and building strong relationships with grantees.
- 80,000 Hours: 80,000 Hours is a non-profit organization that provides career advice for people who want to have a social impact. The organization provides resources and guidance on how to maximize the impact of philanthropic donations.

7.3 Intersection of Sustainable Investing and Philanthropy Resources

Resources that focus on the intersection of sustainable investing and philanthropy can help investors and philanthropists maximize their impact by integrating both approaches. Here are some resources that can help:

- The Impact Management Project (IMP): IMP is a global network of organizations and individuals that provides guidance on impact management. The network includes investors, philanthropists, and other stakeholders who aim to harmon

Conclusion

Sustainable investing and impactful philanthropy are two powerful tools that can be used to drive positive social and environmental change. By understanding how sustainable investing and philanthropy work, and by building sustainable portfolios and measuring impact, individuals and organizations can make a meaningful difference in the world. Use the resources provided in this guide to get started on your journey towards making a positive impact.

Incorporating sustainable investing and impactful philanthropy into our personal and

professional lives can be a rewarding and fulfilling experience. With the knowledge and

resources provided in this comprehensive guide, we can make informed decisions and take

purposeful actions towards creating a more sustainable and equitable future. Remember, small

actions can have a big impact, so don't underestimate the power of your choices. Let's continue

to learn, grow, and work towards a better world for all.

Glossary

Here is a glossary of some important terms and concepts related to sustainable investing and impactful philanthropy covered in this guide:

1. Sustainable Investing: The practice of investing in companies and funds that prioritize environmental, social, and governance (ESG) factors to create long-term value and positive impact.
2. Impactful Philanthropy: The practice of donating time, money, or other resources to organizations or causes with the intention of creating positive social or environmental change.
3. ESG: Environmental, Social, and Governance criteria are a set of standards that investors use to evaluate companies' sustainability and ethical practices.
4. Impact Investing: A type of sustainable investing that seeks to generate measurable, positive social and environmental impact alongside financial returns.
5. Green Bonds: Bonds that are specifically issued to fund projects with environmental benefits, such as renewable energy, energy efficiency, and sustainable water management.
6. Diversification: A risk management strategy that involves investing in a variety of assets and sectors to reduce exposure to any one specific risk.
7. Risk Management: The process of identifying, assessing, and prioritizing risks to minimize their negative impact on investment portfolios.
8. Financial Performance: The return on investment that a portfolio generates over a specific period, often measured against a benchmark or market index.
9. Impact Measurement: The process of assessing and evaluating the outcomes and effectiveness of sustainable investing or philanthropic initiatives.
10. Key Considerations: Factors that investors and philanthropists should take into account when making decisions, such as risk tolerance, values, impact goals, and financial objectives.

www.ingramcontent.com/pod-product-compliance
Lightning Source LLC
Chambersburg PA
CBHW070801220526
45467CB00017B/811